Intimacy

Dellavonte Hune

Ezekiel's World Publishing—Madison, WI
ISBN: 979-8-218-45262-9
Library of Congress Control Number: 2024912764
Title: *Intimacy*
Author: Dellavonte Hune
Digital distribution | 2024
Paperback | 2024

Published in the United States by New Book Authors Publishing

Dedication

In heartfelt dedication, Dellavonte Hune honors his beloved son, Ezekiel Hune-Moss, and the cherished bond they share. As well as his beloved family and friends. For their guidance and support through Hune's journey of life.

1. Ezekiel Hune-Moss
2. Skye Moss
3. Angelica Williams
4. Erica Hune
5. Deontae Spivey
6. Corron Williams
7. Brian McGuire
8. Olive McGuire
9. Fish Family
10. Dj Bell

Table of Contents

Final Thoughts

I've tried to organize the poems into a coherent flow that captures the journey of love - from yearnings and intimacy to the complicated twists and turns, the untangling of deep emotions, turmoil and eventual healing, the bittersweet tapestry of life, and finally two souls becoming intertwined.

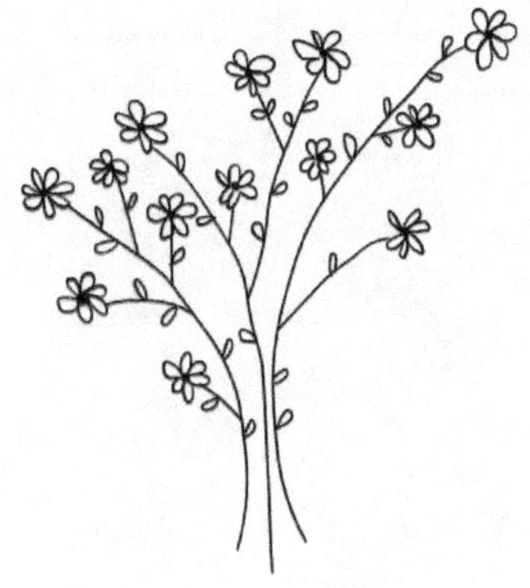

Section 1

Yearnings of the Heart

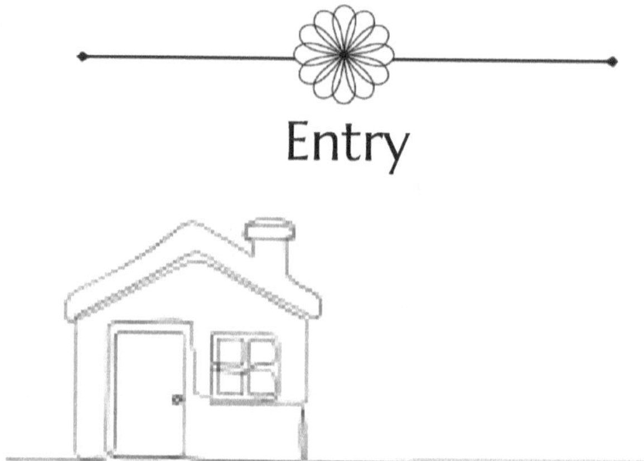

Entry

In this vast tapestry of love's great dance,
A yearning seeks solace in transient romance.
A heart torn betwixt, a yearning unbound,
To love multiple souls, forever spellbound.

For within this soul lies a flame undying,
A hunger for connection, always multiplying.
To taste the nectar of each unique soul,
To embrace their essence, their stories untold.

But how the heart aches, for bonds that entwine,
For a love that is lasting, a love so divine.
To find in one's arms the haven of trust,
A love that transcends, a love that is just.

Yet destiny whispers with bittersweet breath,
That true love's elusive, an enigma of depth.
For some hearts, it seems, are destined to roam,
Seeking love's fragments, far from home.

In the night's embrace, a longing takes flight,
Yearning for intimacy, for love's sweet delight.

But the heart remains restless, forever in chase,
Caressed by many, never settling in one place.

Oh, the joy of each touch, each fleeting affair,
But an ache lingers still, a void to repair.
For in the depths of passion, a whisper is heard,
A melody of longing, an unspoken word.

To find one's soulmate, a love beyond measure,
Where intimacy blooms, unguarded treasure.
To bridge the divide, between passion and peace,
In a love that allows the spirit's release.

But until that day dawns, love's ultimate prize,
The heart continues its search, with hopeful eyes.
Embracing connections, love's beautiful art,
In the tapestry of souls, it finds a home in each part.

A yearning persists, in this love unconfined,
To savor each chapter, each love that aligns.
For in the realm of love, there's room to adore,
Multiple hearts, each one cherished, and more.

So let not the heart be shackled by fear,
Of loving too deeply, of love's vast frontier.
For in the yearning, the wide-open embrace,
We find love's essence, its boundless grace.

May your journey be blessed with love's sweet embrace,
A tale of connections, each one leaving a trace.
And when true love finds you, or you find it, dear friend,
May its embrace be forever, a love without end.

Infusion

To question if I long for her would be like asking the
stars if they ache for the daybreak,
Inquiring if the sun yearns for its golden rays,
Or pondering if the ocean pines for the streams that nourish it.

I've gazed upon the most captivating flowers,
Yet, their scents intertwine like harmonious melodies.
I've wandered through the most breathtaking places on earth,
Yet the wind whispers familiar tunes in every corner.

Only in your presence did the wind carry an elusive aroma to
the flowers,
A fragrance exclusive to that moment.
I'd recognize you in the depths of darkness,
Where you are silent, and I am devoid of sound.

I'd recognize you in another existence,
In varied forms, in disparate epochs,
And I'd adore you through it all,
Until the final star in the sky fades into nothingness.

They inquired, "Do you love her with all your heart?"

I answered, "Speak of her over my resting place, and witness
the revival she brings."

Poetry

I love the way it pours into our ears
Live for the goosebumps it creates

Greener Pastures

In this house, your presence lingers,
In every room, every corner, every shelf,
Memories echo, silent whispers,
Of love that once filled this space, myself.

Tell me, did you feel the change,
As I tried to erase your ghost,
Did you miss the warmth, the familiar range,
Of moments shared and cherished most?

Do you think about me every day,
Long for my touch in the dark of night?
Is the grass truly greener on the other side,
Or does it lack the love we used to ignite?

I'm learning to let go, to set you free,
To release you from the chains I held,
The pain I carry, I understand, you see,
It's time to break the spell you once compelled.

Did you find peace in the break,
Amidst the silence and the tears you cried,
Does my absence haunt your nights awake,
Or have you found a new love, a new stride?

Do you think about me every day,
Long for my touch in the dark of night?
Is the grass truly greener on the other side,

Or does it lack the love we used to ignite?

It's okay to let me go, be free,
To walk away from the pain I bear,
I know the hurt I've caused, you see,
I'll never hurt you or anyone, I swear.

So, leave me, leave the pain behind,
Find the love you seek, the joy untamed,
I'll carry my burden, my love, confined,
And our memories, forever unnamed.

Sky

The sky is falling, but I shouldn't be surprised.
Thought it was an accident, when you came into my life.
Do you see death, when you look into my eyes?

I connected the stars, because I believed they were my guide.
I've never felt so comfortable, having someone by my side.
If I traveled to your dreams, could I see you tonight?

Our moment was like a shooting star, so it's sad to watch it fly by.
I will cherish everyday spent with you, and every night.
Do you believe our stars will align again, in due time?

Beach

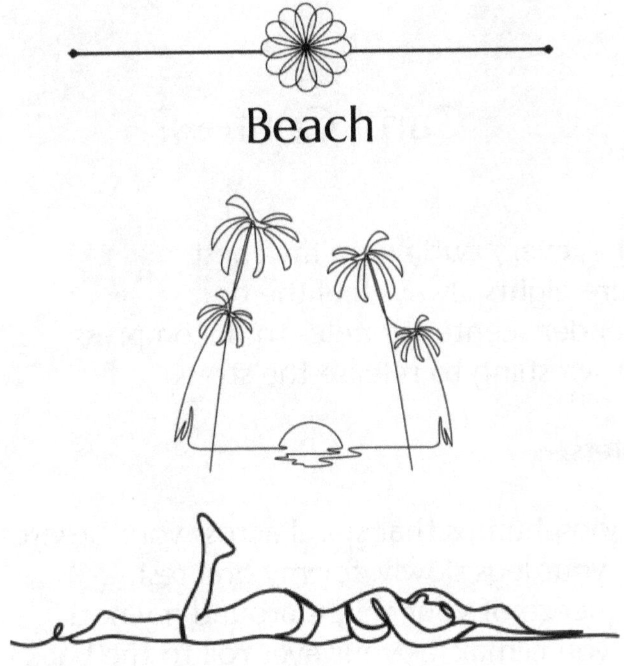

S he wants to be on a beach for the rest of her life
Ain't no surprise, she saw how I was spending my time
Most say, I'm ahead of my prime
Gave her the free pass, jumped ahead of the line

Can I Confess?

Tracing every outline on my chest
Figure eights always feel the best
Lavender scented candles to decompress
Late night wrestling to release the stress

Can I confess?

I kiss the goosebumps that spiral across your breast.
Spreading your legs slowly, for my oral test.
Feel the squeeze of your thighs around my neck.
Watching you climax, as your eyes roll to the back of your head.

Can I confess?

When you're on top, there's no contest
Like when you get aggressive on my neck
Spilling all over my body, but I love the mess
Waited too long, to feel this blessed

Can I confess?
I love this love the best

Can I Call You Later?

In the darkness of the night,
His whispers linger, an eerie delight.
A toxic love, a poison so sweet,
She dances with danger, to his deceit.

His words a spell, his touch a flame,
She's drawn to him, though she feels the shame.
Can I call you later? His voice a lure,
But she knows deep down, his love impure.

In the shadows, he waits for her call,
A puppet master, watching her fall.
His promises empty, his love a lie,
Yet she can't resist, no matter how she tries.

His eyes like fire, his smile a mask,
She's tangled in his web, a difficult task.
Can I call you later? His plea so fake,
But she's under his spell, unable to break.

She knows the danger, she sees the signs,
But love is blind, as she intertwines.
With a toxic man, a poison in disguise,
Can I call you later? His words full of lies.

She longs for freedom, for a love that's true,
But in his web, she's caught askew.
A toxic love, a twisted fate,

Can she break free, before it's too late?

In the silence of the night, she hears his call,
Can I call you later? She stands tall.
No more toxic love, no more deceit,
She walks away, her heart now complete.

Distant Love

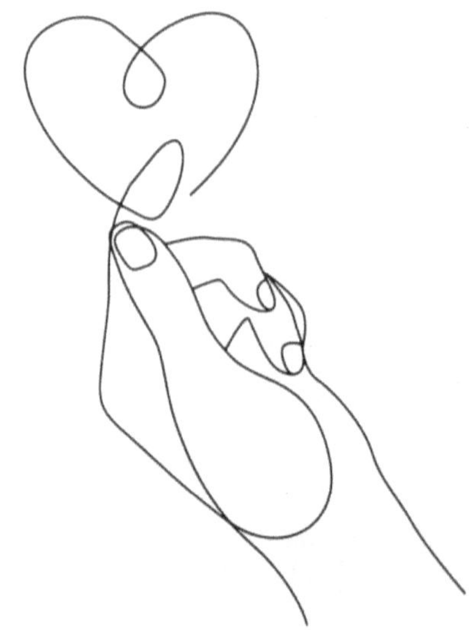

Where we have to be patient
But we can't get enough
Where we have to learn
Before we give up

Distant love

Right Here

You want to do that, right here?
All the talks we won't have, because of that fear
Will only commit to another, when the fog clear
Do you like when I touch you, right there?

What If?

If I told you to come over, would you listen?
Yeah we tried hard, but I don't like this distance.
And I'm not confused, I know my feelings
Stop beating around the bush, who are we kidding?

If I told you it's not over, would you believe it?
Dive off the deep end, even if it meant we were sinking?
These tough, "I miss you's," looking forward to the weekend
But then the week ends, then another week ends, what were
we thinking?

If I told you to come home, would you listen?
Imagine me watching the dishes
Then blowing you kisses, after kisses
Tell me, how much do you miss it?

Do You Still Think About Me?

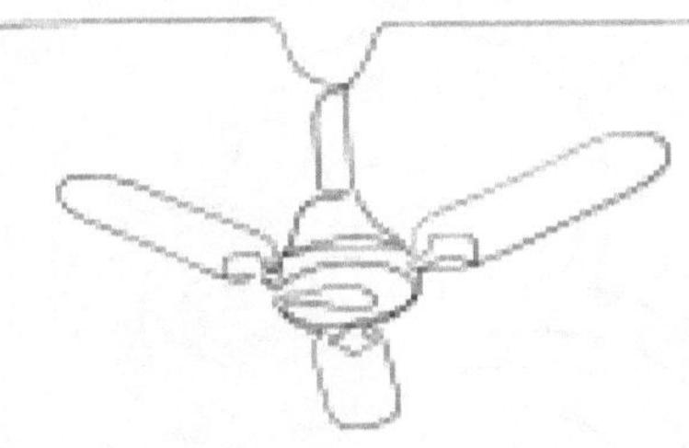

Do you pause when you wake up?
How many times did the fan spin?
Do you still think about me?

Is it hard to go out now?
Heard you dating girls now?
Do you still think about me?

When it rains does it pour?
Is your bad day everyday?
Do you still think about me?

Heard you don't dance no more?
Do you get angry when Brent Faiyaz comes on?
Do you still think about me?

Was it me or was it you?
You done for good now?
Do you still think about me?

Storm

When the storm is here
I can feel the words flooding in
I was just a boy
Didn't know what I was getting in

Thought I could place you in a box
You didn't fit in
They say love will last
But who are we kidding

I placed a seed in the winter snow
I didn't expect for it to grow
Time did past, and what do you know
A flower blossomed, in the winter cold

I loved you then, and I love you now
When it's bright and sunny
Or in the thunders clouds
Because you are me and I'm so fucking proud.

Home

My head's up in the attic
While my heart's in the basement
I'm building up from the pavement
It's our home I'm making

But the house almost caved in
So I had to reinforce the frames that I'm making
It's not THE best creation
But I wanted to show my dedication

We all put up different faces
On the walls that we're pacing
I just hope when days end
It is your face that I'm embracing

Come to Me

World moving too fast, don't even have a moment to take it in
We all drinking the poison, light turns to darkness no one left to save our sins
She said she likes me best once I take off all that flashy stuff and put on a cardigan
Drinking so much, we lose track of what bar we in

Black Love

I want to walk a path with no strings in the back
When I was a kid I wish I lived a life with no skin attached
I want to love on a black Queen, without people saying
"that makes sense" because our skin is black

Greatest Sin

I know I missed your call but I got your text
You went through my phone, so I know you're upset
Collected all my best lines, then laid them like cards on the deck

You screaming so damn hard, I can feel it in my chest
Went through the messages, trying to find the best
What hurt you the most, was your friend that was on top of the list

Now you punching and screaming, acting childish
Asking me how I could be so damn reckless
I planned for it to be you and I, but they came so effortlessly

I'm sorry I couldn't love you properly, but I tried my best

Section 2
Intimacy's Embrace

Take It Slow

When we look at each other, make sure the gaze is soft.
When you speak to me, can it be tempered?
When I speak to you, can you pay attention?
When we touch, I want it to be careful.

Take your time with me.

When we fight, I want to communicate.
When you are angry with me, can you take time to cool off?
When I get angry with you, can you give me time to clear my thoughts?
When we are hurt, I want us to patch each other's wounds.

Take my time with you.

When we take those leaps, let's not move backwards.
When you open up to me, can I accept you?
When I open up to you, can you not run?
When we are weak, let's find strength in vulnerability.

Take our time with this love.

Tryna Be

I know it's hard to see
Screaming through the phone,
"you lied to me!"
I know I said I'd ride for thee,
but it just wasn't in my prophecy.

Honestly, I'm afraid of "honesty."
Because the truth won't make you proud of me.
So it is, what it got to be.
Moving in silence, is the only option for me.

But I might as well tell you, what you're bound to see.
Video Vixen's hanging all over me.
Virtual OPs watching my story, so closely.
Just hoping one day I can make you proud of me.

For now, I'm tryna be, everything they said I be.

Strangers to Lovers

If you flip a coin, you get one of two choices

Love You Naked

Expressing love and acceptance for someone in their most vulnerable state can be a beautiful sentiment. It's about appreciating and cherishing the person for who they truly are, without any masks or pretenses. When you say "love you naked," it can mean that you love and accept them completely, flaws and all.

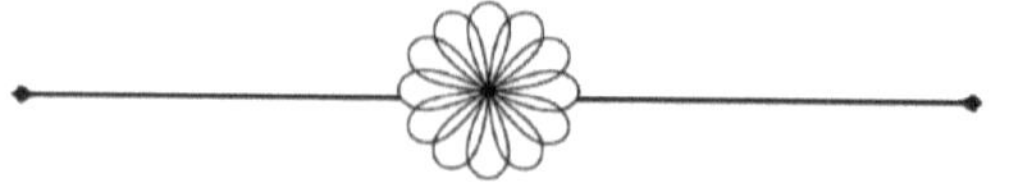

Strength in Vulnerability

It's like I'm falling, falling deep
When I say I love you, imagine me on my knees
Thanking God he gave me the vision to see

Lost in thought, imagining wild fantasies
Only skin to skin, when you next to me
When I hear your thoughts, that's the best intimacy

If I say I'm yours, will you stay with me?
I had to patch my heart, because it started to bleed
I want to be stronger, than I use to be

Waited my whole life to feel this peace
So when I get you, I don't want you to leave
I want you to find strength in vulnerability, when you look at
me

Fruitful Life

All the kidding a side, I got a fruitful life
Abundance of money, and a whip that's tinted real nice
So far ahead of these dudes that nothing can catch me by surprise

Shorty gripping that iron, and watching my sides
Roll those windows down, and hit you two times
She shooting while I drive

She's Bonnie and I'm Clyde
That's why the foreign, only fits two inside
It's a do or die, but it's forever you and I

What a fruitful life

Vibez

She likes the taste, because I smell like coco butter and weed.
You got to climb the trees with the slick branches, if you want to catch the breeze
Trying to slide between those legs and bless her, every time she sneeze

I drop a coin and collect her gum balls
I guess money is the only thing, that get her on her knees
Two seater, nice Beamer, that's why she loves to ride on me

Slick talk with a nice walk, got her begging "baby please!"
Sweet wine mixed with smooth vibes, now I got her in the sheets
Hot girl summer is over for you, I guess you stuck with me

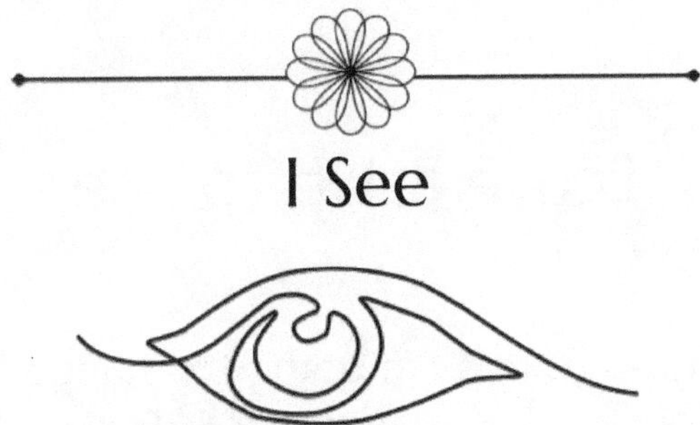

I See

see behind all the angry text.
A scared girl under distress.
I see behind the self love posts.
A soul looking for a soul to call home.

I see behind the "you're blocked" messages on the screen.
A person so desperate to be seen.
I see behind all the tight clothes.
You don't want anybody, just that somebody to hold.

I see behind the tears.
Drowned in makeup so the image is never clear.
I see behind the pain.
Stuck in the streets but trying to get out of this game.

I see behind the hurt.
Mishandled so much that your pride is on alert.
It's like you lost a family member, the way your heart is plastered on your shirt.

You've been hit so you ready to shoot back.
Letting a man treat you like his "Queen" with no strings attached.
No doubling back, if they had you and they left you, ain't no coming back.
If they want your love there's rules attached and energy to match.

I see you.

Leave It Up to Me

If you leave it up to me, I'm going to change the cycle
Kissing on your neck, you love me BAD like Michael
Lay you down on your back, and kiss it with my eyes close

Going through my phone at night
seeing old numbers back at the top again, I guess I love to recycle
You call me the devil reincarnate, have you questioning the Bible

Every time we link, the spirit lift up inside you
I think you might be obsessed with me, tracking everything I do
"Daddy just like that!" Have your soul on revival

Leave it up to me, and watch what I do.

Keep That Between Us

All the banter and tiptoeing
All the unspoken meet ups
All the times our hands grazed passed each other
Keep that between us

All those late nights smoking in my car
All those weird dates, just to spend time together
All those moments that were missed
Keep that between us

All the places we were supposed to go
All the people we were supposed to make jealous
All the memories we were supposed to make
Keep that between us

Stars in the Darkness

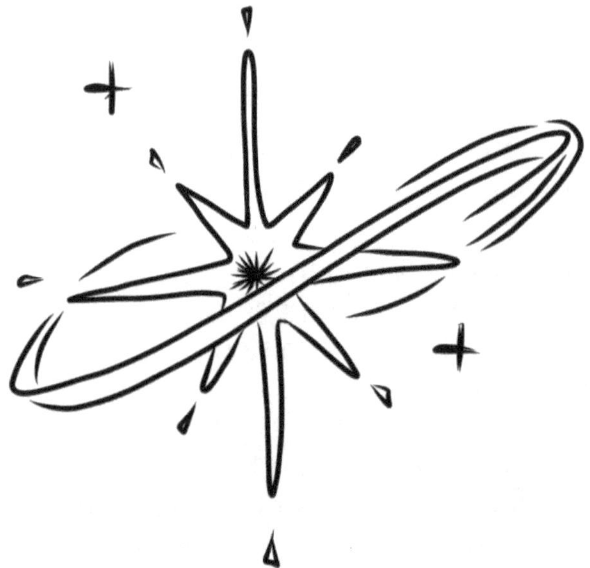

In the stillness of the night, they shine,
Those stars within the darkness, mine.
Love, a madness that consumes whole,
Body, heart, and soul in lovers' role.

Gates unlocked, treasures laid bare,
Hoping they'll cherish scars, not just what's fair.
Each love a birth, a star aglow,
In the depths of darkness, a radiant show.

Love's light recalls a time gone by,
Before the darkness claimed the sky.
Humanity remembered in love's embrace,
A smile for the stars, in time and space.

In the tapestry of memories, they gleam,
Those stars of love, like a lucid dream.
Gazing at the constellations I hold dear,
Each star a testament to all I hold near.

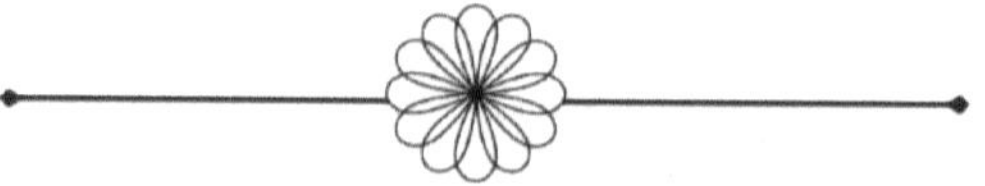

Heaven in Her Thighs

In the midst of chaos, I found peace,
A heaven in her, where my soul found release.
Through trials and tribulations, we fought,
But in her arms, I found the sanctuary I sought.

Her touch ignites a fire deep within,
A passion so intense, it's almost a sin.
In her eyes, I see a love so true,
A connection so deep, it feels brand new.

We faced storms and weathered the tide,
But in her love, I found a place to hide.
She's the queen of my heart, my ultimate prize,
In her love, I find solace and rise.

In her embrace, I find my truth,
Lost in the moment, in the passion, in the youth.
She's my heaven on earth, my guiding light,
In her arms, I find my endless night.

So here we stand, blessed and free,
In the haven of her love, just her and me.
Together we conquer, together we thrive,
In her love, I find my reason to survive.

Silhouette

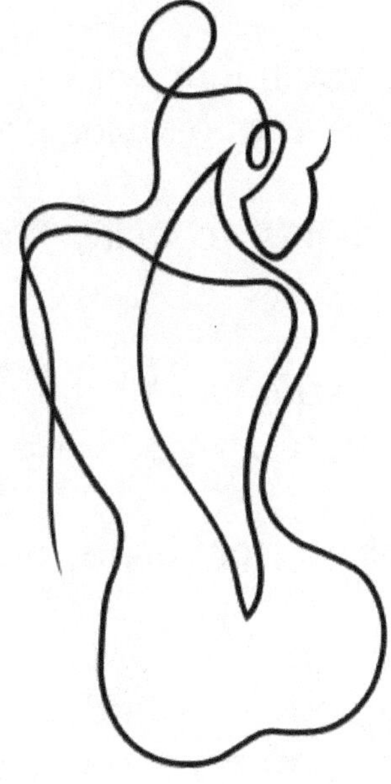

I love when you're on top, during a full moon.
Outlining your silhouette in the moonlight
I watch you embrace the power

You May Not/But I Do

Life moves fast, so you might not catch the picture
Might take a few years of partying, to admit you truly miss her
Blinded by the flashy lights, to many fans asking you to kiss her

You might stumble, on your way to the top of the mountain
learned too much success, will make you feel like you drowning
So many people asking for hand outs, got your head pounding

Blurry pictures all you post, so nobody copy the blueprint
Driving around in that twenty twenty something with the blue tints, because the streets crowded
There was a lot of anxiety, sleepless nights, and pretty girls to keep you grounded

They may not know where you headed, but I do I do I do

Can I Call You Rose

Can I call you Rose?
   Cause you're beautiful and dangerous at the same
   time
Where you can grab her, but she'll leave a mark behind
Yet she only needs a little watering to survive

Can I call you Rose?
Cause you're the balance between elegance and Devine
Where the beginning and the end intertwine
Yet you have to love her with your limited time

Can I call you Rose?
Cause I want to celebrate you like you were a gift of mine
Where love meets it's final demise
Yet, even when it's dead I will cherish you until the end of time

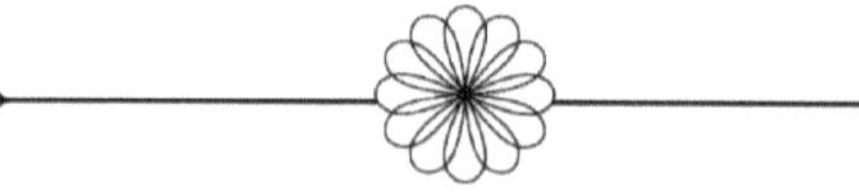

Last Call

I want to be your smile in the morning
I want to be your comic relief
I want to be your groovy dance partner
I want to be your chauffeur home

I want to be that last shot
I want to be that tempting name in your phone
I want to be that bad habit
I want to be that favorite addiction

I need to be the air to your lungs
I need to be the only options
I need to be the reason why
I need to be the number you dial when the bar says, "last call."

Flaws

It's hard not to find flaws in people
But I love everything about you
And I know it's hard to believe
Not to find one negative thing in someone

Yet it's true, I am utterly and completely in love with
everything about you.
And it scares the hell out of me, having so much love
towards another soul

Tearing through layer after layer, after layer
And still finding that layer more beautiful than the last

Like a blossoming flower

But I'm scared.... Scared that my skeletons might be too
frightening to look at
Scared that my demons maybe too loud for your ears
Scared that you might pick at my flaws and throw me away
like raisins in the sun

I guess I'm a child still at the core, scared of the world scared
of acceptance.

So, I'm sorry if my cold exterior pushes you away
It's only here to protect the last bit of innocence I have left

Fragile Not Weak

She said she's fragile not weak
The cover reads different from what you can see
Love and loyalty is all she needs
Doesn't need a baller, rather have me down on one knee

Whenever she's in trouble, she can count on me
Pull up and start spraying, hit'em 1-2-3
"My nigga can get crazy, when it comes to me."
Joker and Harley Quinn, how we roam the streets

Don't talk a lot, my ears is all I need
Hustle and consistency is what she sees
Sex and no stress, is all we breathe
Treat her like she's fragile, but I'd never call her weak.

Section 3
Love's Complicated Dance

Progress Not Perfection

I choose progress not perfection
Cause I gain so much more in these lessons
I find humility, knowledge and reference
Through patience I discovered blessings

I don't want you done, I want you in the making
Can't get complacent, got to make progress before the day ends.
Cut out the distractions, and focus on the void
You start to see light at the end of the tunnel, when you cut out all the noise

Let's not get frantic, I want you to have poise
Find comfort in being uncomfortable, so try not to avoid

to recoil.
The journey of progress, a path we embark,
Seeking growth and learning, leaving a lasting mark.
Perfection may beckon, a tempting notion to chase,
But in its pursuit, shadows can cloud our space.

Instead, progress we choose, with its gifts so grand,
Humility, knowledge, and wisdom at hand.
With patience as our guide, we uncover hidden treasures,
Unveiling blessings in life's simplest pleasures.

Polar Opposites

In the chaos of our love, we stand apart
Polar opposites, yet bound by same beating heart
You speak in words, I in actions and deeds
Our love languages clash, planting unwanted seeds

In moments of silence, I ponder all the pain
I've caused you with my actions, again and again
Your love language, so foreign to me
I struggle to understand, but I long to see

The hurt in your eyes, the sorrow in your voice
Remind me that I must make a different choice
To learn your language, to bridge the divide
To show you my love, to stand by your side

For we may be different, but somehow the same
Complementary pieces in this love game
You speak with your heart, I with my soul
Opposites attract, making us whole

So I'll strive to do better, to speak your love tongue
To cherish and honor, for our love has just begun
For though we may be polar opposites, it's true
It's the very thing that makes me perfect for you.

Should've Stayed Home

Getting all fancy, because you grown now

Moving so damn fast, ain't no use in slowing down

So many gave you up, so you used to being alone now

Taking care of your drunk friends, got you thinking "I should go home now."

Constantly being told you wrong, got you feeling like you in a dog pound

Driving drunk while it's pouring out

One false move got you swearing now

In the matter of seconds, cut the lights out

Should've stayed home

Know You So Well

You love to shop, at the wholesale.
Like cheap vacations, staying up at the motel.
Racing home stating, "I got something to share but please don't tell."

Know you so well.

Staying in on the weekends like a hermit with no shell.
Hate long goodbyes, and farewells.
Don't do dating apps, because you're convinced that men are "unwell."

Know you so well.

Know the words to whisper in detail.
Only need one hand, like Odell.
Have your body shaking, listening to Miguel.

I know you so well.

Never Been Scared

I've never been scared of deep waters, raging fires nor
earthquakes, but I'm scared of you

The eyes of stardust that stand for eternity
The skin that dances like sunlight and gives life
The voice of a song that I have heard in many lives before
The touch that silenced my most deafening demons

I've never been scared of struggle, defeat nor the spotlight,
but I'm scared of you

The eyes of sorrow from a lost land
The skin that wears battle scars like medals
The voice that bellows for racial justice
The touch that remains soft even after mistreatment

I've never been scared of intimacy, solitude nor dying alone,
but I'm scared to love you

Twists & Turns

She likes the fight, calls it dancing
I like when she bites, call it dining out
We like to react, sexual tension when the glass cracks
Twists and turns

She likes when I'm on my knees, begging her please
I like when she undresses slowly, feel the rise when she tease
We like the game, handle it with ease
Twists and turns

She loves when she can feel it coming
I love when she spills all over me
We love the slow rise, to the release
Twist and turns

Nobody but You

Me: Why we always have to argue at a party? I hate when you get on Bacardi

Her: I thought you liked, when I'm wild and naughty. Or that must've been your other shorty?

Me: She would have acted right, imagine it now.... Hmmm, what a beautiful sight.

Her: You only saying shit, to start a fight. But that's alright, got another that'll treat me right.

Me: Might have another, but it don't feel as tight. Lord knows, he ain't hitting it right.

Her: What are we even doing, you don't care about nobody??!

Me: Nobody but you.

Silent car ride

Her: You like the way I look....?
Me: I admire the way the sun, catches beauty off your skin.

Her: You don't mind my size?

Me: I love to outline your curves, like the stroke of a paint brush on a new canvas.

Her: You like how I taste?

Me: With every bite, my hungry grows. Seconds wouldn't be enough, I need 3rds, 4ths, 5ths. Well, you get the point.

Her: You want to grow old together?

Me: One life time wouldn't be enough. I need forever with you.

Her: You love me?

Me: I love the air you breathe, the ground you step on, and God himself. For blessing this world, with you. So, yes I love you.

Her: But you don't care about nobody?

Me: Nobody but you.

Judgement Day

I stand before you, different than I once was.
With attentions much different, than they once were.
Words much harsher, than they used to be.

Poetic expression of love, turning into battle scars.
Devotions spewing from our mouths, sound more rhetorical
with time.
Fruit that was once sweet, tasting more sour with every bite.

I stand before you today, no longer an ally but an enemy.
No longer love concealed in my eyes, but tears my darling.
A grip once tight, loosened until non-existent.

Plans of our future, turned into plans of my own.
The house once built, now demolished with no trace.
Love that was birthed in our hearts, now known as distant
dreams.

I stand before you today, different.
Once upon a time I was your lawyer, your savior.
Now your judge, and with the evidence before us.

I cast judgement and fair ruling.

First One to Win

It has been a race since I met you.
The truth is, I shouldn't have ever left you.
Caught up on what it was, didn't know how to express
what I went through.
In turn, I started to neglect you.

I've been running for a thousand miles.
The feeling of being chased, haunted me since I was a child.
Darkness crept in, and it stayed a while.
You could hear it in my voice, the echo so vile

When we started to race, I started regaining the taste.
Companionship right in my face, with a soft embrace.
But was it fake or did I make a mistake?
Here I thought the chase was to the end, not a love race.

So I did everything I could, to shut you out.
Screams of insecurity, plagued me with doubt.
Stuck in a man's body, but internally a child.

It has been a race since I met you, but I don't want to run
now.

This a Poem Not a Rap

This a poem not a rap
All these dudes do is get on the media and cap
All the shit they say they doing, but ain't bringing you facts
All on live flashing they shortys racks
You must be a spilled bottle, the way they giving you cap

But I'd never dim your potential, and you can find peace in that
With everyone trying to hold you where you are, I inspire to level you up from where you at
Ain't no competition with me, we can both be the boss, there's plenty of room for that

I'm talking you on top, then I'm on top, we can play pitty pat
A pretty Beamer two seater, leave our luggage where it's at, because there's no room for that
So just relax, let me feed that body and mind, with no strings attached
Break that spine, love you right, and that's the end of that

Wildfire

You were born to ignite, there was no safety.
Spreading like gasoline, on my lungs lately.
How that burn makes me think of you daily.

Clouds fill the room, smoke smelling like sage baby.
Ash in my throat, but that was part of the deal you gave me.
Breathes becoming short, do you think you could save me?

I think I rushed in too fast, you should have paced me.
Sprinting to the end, I see you're trying to race me.
Wildfire in my heart, I don't know why love fucking hates me.

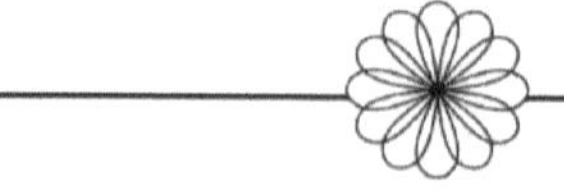

Beautiful Lies

R ose buds blooming off your lips
Soil soaked between your thighs
Love to hold it and look me in my eyes
Beautiful lies

Feel most comfortable when you ride it
On top of the world when I'm inside it
Bite your lips, trying to hide it
Beautiful lies

See the passion when we fighting
Sentences sound muffled cause you crying
Screaming you love me, to the sky
Beautiful lies

Talk 2 U

Darkness grows over her, silently creeping
Death tries to take over her, violently deep in
Her body laying all over him, she's finally sinking
They can't survive in the deep end

He never hears her side, so she's always on defense
She don't trust his friends, cause they all quietly cheating
Caught him in a lie, the truth finally seeps in
She done found his weakness

She so done with his ass, she just needed a reason
Nails done, hair done, she already prepared for the weekend
All on Instagram shaking ass, knowing her man is probably tweaking
He called about 20 times, no hesitation when she declines, all her friends started geeking
We all look forward to the weekend.

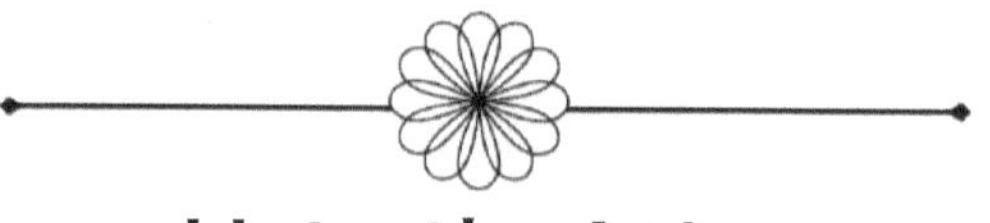

Hate the Way

Darling, I hate the way you love me,
It's like a tempest raging, a storm upon the sea.
Your love's a fierce warrior, battle-hardened and true,
Braving the raging tides, fighting through and through.

It's scars we bear, etched deep within our souls,
From the battles we've fought, and the stories left untold.
But your love's a fortress in the chaos, a beacon in the dark,
An anchor in my storm, the home within my heart.

I take it back, I don't hate the way you love,
In fact, every trial endured, made our bond rise above.
Your love's a warrior's anthem, a battle cry so real,
And I'll face any storm with you, with a love that I now feel.

All I Do Is Love You

Seems like everything I do, gets shot down
Best man you've ever had, but you don't want no man now
My love is trying to break free, but you just want it in the dog pound

Must be on a ferris wheel, the way we going round and round
Said she's tired of the arguments, and the up and downs
Only way to find peace, is if we both give up now

Send my love off to the sky, and pray it never comes down
Shape shifting, everything you said I was I am now
The truth is you're no better than what you allow

Out Here

Out here people do what they want.
Staying out all night, don't care what it cost.

Out here people want a good time.
No off roading, just stay in their lane.

Out here people drink insane.
Champagne showers, helps them forget the pain.

Out here people are empty.
Everyone on their solo mission,
No time for love to get in the way.

Out here there are fallen angels.
Lost in this flesh of skin.
Trying to find their way home.
Trying to find the promise land.

Tell Me You Need Me

The fire that burns within me, it yearns to hear you say,
That you need me by your side, every step and every day.
There's an ache within my soul, a longing that won't
cease,
To bask in the warmth of your love, to find in you my peace.

Tell me you need me, in your arms to hold you tight,
Let your words be my shelter, on the darkest of nights.
For in the symphony of your voice, I find a soothing balm,
Assuring me that in your heart, I'll always find my calm.

I crave the sweet whispers of love, to calm my restless fears,
To know that in your heart, I've held and kept my years.
So tell me you love me, with every breath you take,
For in your constant reassurance, my doubts will surely break.

The Danger of Her Love

I've faced lions and bears, even guns and wars,
But there's one fear that rattles me to my very core.
It's not the danger of man, nor nature's raw might,
But the love of a certain woman, that keeps me up at night.

Her love, it's like a storm, stirring something deep within,
Unleashing fears and feelings, like a wild reckless spin.
It's not her anger that scares me, nor her fierce, fiery gaze,
But what her love might reveal, in those vulnerable, tender
ways.

To stand tall in her love, and face what it may stir,
Is a courage I need to find, to let myself be sure.
In her love lies a power I can't easily ignore,
A love so strong, it shakes me to my very core.

Tell Me Why I'm waiting

When you said it was over, I didn't believe it
Cause we bragged about all the things we'd be achieving
I guess you didn't inform me about your little secret
And when you left, it felt like I was stuck in the deep end

In the darkness alone, I couldn't believe it
Left me trapped with all my demons
I can hear them cackling and creeping
Consumed by it all I can feel myself sinking

Pinch me now, I have to be dreaming
Take the bottle away, I shouldn't be doing all this drinking
Must have a "free love" sign on me, the way you be taking
If you already gone, why the fuck am I still waiting?

Please Don't Leave

I see my leaves are falling
Blowing through the breeze
If you had one more token
Would you spend it on me?

Spent my whole life fighting
So I need you to be my peace
If the image still blurry
Here's my glasses, now you see

Seeing visions of us intertwined
Call that love therapy
Before I fully commit to love
I just have one more thing

Please don't leave

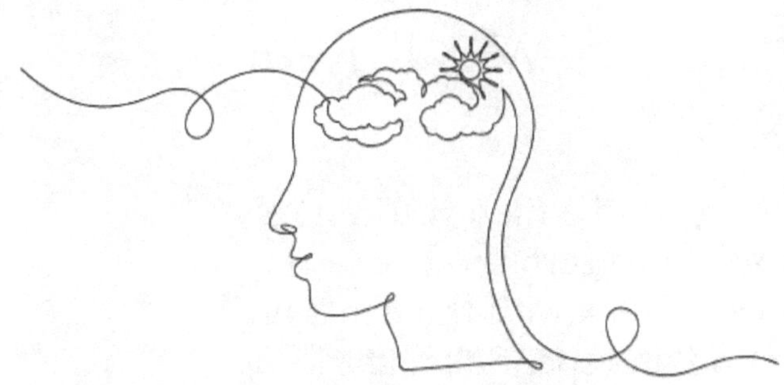

Section 4

Untangling the Emotions

Was It Real

Said you needed a man you can rely on
Roll a wood to turn the vibes on
You love to fuck with the lights on
Fucked around and spent all night long
Was it real?

Miss the days we were in different time zones
FaceTime all day, attached to you like a hip bone
Driving all night, swerving through the back roads
Get to you, make sure that back gone
Was it real?

Can't pinpoint when we started fighting
All those days we felt divided
Put on mask and started lying
Our connection slowly dying
Was it real?

Different Day Same Agenda

We are in different times, yet we face the same obstacles
I love you I hate you, yeah we hear a lot of those
I hug you, then rub you, then fuck you, call it our nightly ritual
We make love instead of communicating, it's starting to become habitual

Seems like the canvas creates the same image, regardless if we use different strokes
Walking around each other, hiding our truth, we put on different coats
We want to so desperately sing the same song, but we on different flows
Therapist told us to jot down why we love one another, but we both came with different notes

She said, "I can't do this anymore," and that's all she wrote

Summertime

Four seasons, but you're my favorite time of the year
Back road driving, so the vision ain't so clear
Long nights and many cities, just trying to make it home
to you my dear

And I know we have our fuses and our fights be so severe
Storming out the house when I should have treated you like
my peer
Never forgave myself that night, when I saw you shed those
tears

Yet our bond last forever, doesn't matter who meet around
this sphere
And I know I get emotional, when I have one too many beers
But I got you like you got me, 365 days out of the year

Some Flowers Bloom

Some flowers out there bloom and grow
Water feeds the seeds and the sun watches them grow
But not for you and not for me
We just boom and let go, big explosion

Some flowers drift away from this game
The wind carries them away to the ocean
But not for you and not for me
We get stuck in our game, we stay frozen

Some flowers have their hands out
Looking for someone who will save them
But not for you and not for me
We can't show our vulnerable side, it's too dangerous

She said, "You don't water me anymore."
I said, "You don't let me breathe anymore."

Some flowers bloom and grow and let go to the open
Not for you and not for me, we are hopeless

WY@

Where you at? Got a lot I want to talk about
You know the streets talk, they like to run they mouth
Dusse got me acting up, currently outside your momma's house
Men's nem said they saw you with another, but the timeline don't make sense
So I'm just trying to work it out

Was supposed to be a girls night out on the town
Whole time you were at his house
Caked up watching Netflix, on his couch
Texted you that night but you said, "there was nothing to worry about."

Had me feeling crazy, plagued my mind with all kinds of doubts
Said I'm insecure, but that was your way of trying to find an out
If you weren't feeling a nigga, we could have figured out another route

Now I'm back outside on the daily
Got bitches on my line driving me crazy
One of them said they pregnant, and they having my baby
Been numb for awhile, so shit didn't faze me
Drinking too much, my mind getting hazy

Where you at? I need you to come save me

Your Soul, Trust Me, I Got You

Let me reconnect to disconnect
I must see the deepest parts of you
Your dreams your fears
Your soul

May I reconnect to disconnect?
Let me hold your insecurities
Place them in my hands
Trust me

Must we always reconnect to disconnect?
We have to get to work
If you're scared, don't worry
I got you

Hurt

Things are different than before
Watched you walkout that door
Once, my heart was pure
But I don't love you anymore

Now I hear the storm louder than before
Hear that wind, feel the rain pour
The cold sinks in more and more
I can feel it through my core

Can't move on because I'm sore
Addicted to that love galore
I ran you out, that's for sure
Now I'm drowning, on the shore

Until the Morning

I've been losing some sleep, could be one of two things
Clouds of smoke, with bottle girls pouring casamigos on me
Or maybe it's all the tussling we've been doing, got us turning the sheets

Kissing your collarbone, while you kissing my cheek
The temperature starting to rise, I think you might be stuck with me
This the promise we keep

Don't you go to sleep
Working our way from the kitchen, now I have you on the bathroom sink
Got you thinking all these dudes are lame, cause they can't fuck with me
We only here until the morning, so you gone stay up with me

Perfect For Somebody Else

In the mirror, I see your reflection,
A masterpiece crafted with my affection.
I shaped you, molded you to perfection,
But now you're ready for a new connection.

I painted your flaws with my tainted brush,
Smoothed out your edges, gave you a hush.
I made you perfect, flawless, no rush,
Now you're set free, with a new crush.

I whispered lies, sweet words in your ear,
Made you believe I was the only one here.
But now you see clear, without a tear,
You're polished and shining, no longer near.

I dressed you up in love's deceiving guise,
Masked your truth with my toxic lies.
I made you perfect in someone else's eyes,
A masterpiece now, to my demise.

Internet Girl

In the digital world, I met this Internet Girl,
A material essence in a flashy whirl.
Yearning for lights, not a heart to hold,
Seeking validation from a screen, cold.

Mesmerized by her beauty, I stand in awe,
Her allure casting a captivating draw.
Spellbound by her charm, lost in her gaze,
Drowned in her world, trapped in her maze.

She craves the spotlight of virtual affection,
Leaving me longing for a real connection.
Yet, I linger entangled in her enchanting spell,
Caught in her web, where love doesn't dwell.

Internet Girl, a modern-day muse,
Leaving me tangled in emotions to choose.
With every click, I fall deeper in lust,
A toxic attraction, lost in her virtual dust.

In the realm where pixels reign supreme,
I'm but a shadow in her vanity dream.
Yearning for love, her heart remains closed,
Internet Girl, a tale of a love deposed.

If The World Was Ending

In the hush of twilight's subtle sigh,
As the world's end softly draws near,
My queen, in this timeless heartbeat,
Would you, love, shed all fear?

In the melody of a fading sky's song,
Will you journey to where my soul resides?
To dance with me in the last notes of time,
And in our shared silence, let love abide?

When the stars gently bow out of sight,
And the universe bids its final adieu,
Will you, my heart, in this tender light,
Choose to be the last, so I can make it home to you?

For in this delicate balance of grace,
I crave the rhythm of your touch within,
To stand, hand in hand, in the face of fate,
And let our eternal love begin.

So tell me, in this story's final scene,
When we're miles away, and too much space in between.
Would you chase me down, like a fading dream?

Jealous

In the realm of love's embrace, I pen a verse,
Of envy's shade that lingers all too near.
For in their hearts, a flame glows, aflame, immersed,
While I, in shadows, clutch at doubt and fear.

Oh, how they bask in radiant self-discovery,
Confident, like blossoms kissed by dawn's first light,
Each step they take, they dance with boundless glee,
While echoes of my regrets dim my sight.

Like a distant star, their self-love shines,
A beacon of grace and self-assurance,
With every breath, their confidence entwines,
A melody of strength, devoid of pretense.

They whisper love to their reflections,
While I falter in the depths of my own gaze,
Their hearts aflame with gentle affections,
A symphony of self-love's gentle praise.

In their eyes, I yearn to find that missing link,
A mirror that reflects my worth and grace,
To love myself as they love themselves, I think,
In this journey, I long to find my place.

But listen, dear soul, hear my gentle plea,
For we are bound by threads invisible and strong,
Love for oneself is a path, whispered secretly,
How can we walk it if we doubt our song?

Where Truth & Trust Meet

Within love's eternal waltz, our souls entwine
Truth whispers sweet melodies of romance.
Belief in the depths where hearts align,
Guiding souls to a love divine.

In the quiet chambers of the heart's reflection,
Trust blooms like a rare, precious collection.
Actions speak louder than words so true,
Binding us in a love that forever grew.

Through the trials of time and test,
In love's embrace, we find our rest.
For where truth's belief and trust's action intertwine,
A love so deep, a love so fine.

In your eyes, I see the spark of truth,
In your touch, I feel the trust of youth.
Together we weave a love so pure,
For in your arms, my heart is sure.

So let us walk this path hand in hand,
Where truth and trust eternally stand.
In love's embrace, we find our connection,
A bond forged in love, our eternal affection.

Rebirth

As the earth burns through the ground
The last of the candles have burned out
Hollow echoes, no one's left in this old town

Cracks Beneath the Surface

What does sorry mean, without a resolution?
Why try to lead, if we don't know what we are doing?
When will we be honest, and admit we are clueless?
How can we be growing, if it feels like we're losing?

What will it take, for all of it to break?
Why can't we hold each other, whenever we are in a fight?
When will we pass this painful point of life?
How can we heal, if we don't want to hear the other side?

What can we do, with each decision, we pay the price?
Why doesn't the lord say shit, when we pray to the sky?
When will we cave and put our pride to the side?
How will it shatter, a million cracks being traced between the lines?

Brown Skin 2.0

In the golden glow of evening, her skin aglow,
Smooth as silk, a radiant brown that steals the show.
Her curves, a masterpiece, sculpted by the sun's embrace,
Leaving me longing to be skin to skin, in an eternal embrace.

Captivated by her essence, a yearning deep and true,
Wanting to unravel every layer, immersed in the hue.
Her body a canvas of desire, a work of divine art,
A landscape I ache to explore, where she's the beating heart.

Lost in the fantasy of laying intertwined, forevermore,
In the tender warmth of her presence, my spirit would soar.
Her smooth brown skin, a heavenly sight in the sun's soft ray,
A craving to hold her close, to never let her slip away.

Yet in the longing, there's a melody of bittersweet,
A desire that dances with the ache when we don't meet.
But in the depths of yearning, there's a song yet to be sung,
A love that whispers secrets, where hearts and bodies become one.

Section 5
Turmoil and Healing

What Have I Done

I spoke the words into existence
She catches me in deep thought, when I'm reminiscing
Red lipstick on my neck, she asked, "who are you kissing."
Absent thoughts, love is gone, what am I missing?

I touched you, now a flower grows
Will it blossom or wither, no one knows
Trying to build our own path, but the road is already choose
She says let's take one more trip, one more chance, let's see
how it goes

It all started with fun
The excitement has only begun
Our love is on the run
Dear lord, what have I done?

Calling For You

Staring at Your number, like a lottery ticket
Go together like gas & a spark, we always catch fire when you trippin
Cold case files, they always get denied, cause the way you be slippin
"Cheater on a trial," good thing I got a jury and a witness

Don't get too pretentious, there's a lot I ain't even mention
There's a baby and two baby fathers in the mixes
I ain't mad at you though, you're here and then you're gone you always stay switching
But you set the spark and I get burned, it's like the devil stay winning

Yet I still have your name in my phone with a heart, like a deadly addiction
Been too long since I seen you, and I need my fixes
Even with a knife in my back, I look up to the sky and starting blowing you kisses
Calling for you, but I got to call my lawyer for permission

Hate & Love

Most nights don't feel the same.
Only a few hearts feel the pain.
Love and hate, is the same game.
But both are hard to maintain.

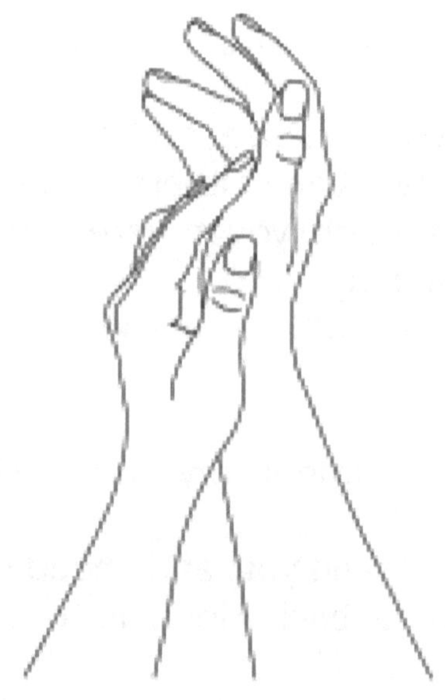

Vision Girl

I want to break out of these walls you see
You're my vision girl, you're my fantasy
Held you in the clouds, looking so heavenly
I gave you my heart, and you ran like a thief

Yeah you left me, broken down you see
I had a vision, but you crushed my dreams
You took the ring off, you had enough of me
You packed everything up, I had to watch you leave

Yeah I had to watch you leave
And you had to watch me bleed
I was crying out, but you didn't hear a thing
You on the road now, you on the go now
No chance to hear me out, cause that's in the past now

I Could

I could count stars, with the sight you give me
Move mountains, with the encouragement you whisper in my ear
Speak hope to a barren land, with the way you touch me
Live to forever, with the life you breathe into me

I could rewrite history, with the memories of us
Cure sickness, with the left over love we created
Win the lottery, with you as my prize
Breathe for the first time, with you as my air

I could heal our past, with the direction you give
Storm through the darkness, with the light you bring
Jump off the edge, with you as my parachute
Die and revive, with you as my pulse

I could change the world, with you by my side

All Because of You

My name doesn't sound the same.
Dreams and passions sound lame.
None of the smiles hide the pain.

All because of you.

Heart suffers so much it's blain.
Thought I was ready for you in fain.
Built this life for us, all in vain.

All because of you.

I'm stuck in this never ending game.
Clout chasers only wanting the fame.
Blind eyes see more than pain, expressions on heads look so feign.

On the Run

On the run from myself
Stuck in my head and it's bad for my health
Never felt fair with the cards I was dealt
And I never told you once, because I didn't want you to feel
what I felt

On the run from time
Lost in memories trapped in my mind
Actions were so lethal but the words were so kind
Held you so damn tight never wanted you to leave my side

On the run from you
One false move and I blew
Rage in your eyes too
So much stacked against us what could we do

Did It to Yourself

What more can I say? You played in my face
Had visions of you walking down that isle
Now I see the door slamming behind you, as you
walking out my place
Guess it was never ending that way

You did it to yourself, you didn't need no help
Had my heart out, but the cold is all it felt
Told me I needed therapy, and time by myself
But I know all that lashing out was cries for help

All this arguing we doing is bad for our health
Trying to kick me while I'm down, when you already won the
belt
And I wish those hateful words is all I felt
Saw all the signs, so I guess I did it to myself

Love Is

Rubbing you when we go to bed
Morning kisses with bad breath
Cleaning you in the shower

Love is

Whipping me up breakfast before work
Making sure I take my vitamins in the morning
Extra kisses and affirmations before we part ways

Love is

Arguments where there is resolutions
Obstacles that we have to get through
Building from the platform we created

Love is
You
Love is
Me
Love is
Us

Gathered the Pieces

I gathered the pieces
You said that you hate me, I hope you didn't mean it
Emotions change like the seasons
Caught in the lies, now I'm trapped in the deep end

What was I thinking
Said I had problems, must be my demons
Got my pride on the defense
Yet, I'm the one who broke us, so I have to gather the pieces

Apology

To you, my love, these words I send,
A humble plea, a heart to mend.
With remorseful heart and soul contrite,
I pen this apology, guided by light.

In deepest realms of my regret,
I saw my errors, a tale of neglect.
Blinded by pride, I failed to see,
The pain I caused, unintentionally.

I apologize for not being there,
To lend my strength, your burdens to share.
In those moments of darkness and despair,
I should have listened, showed you I care.

As you poured your heart, your tears, your fears,
I turned a blind eye, ignored your tears.
My silence echoed upon your pleas,
A stinging wound, unfelt disease.

But now I see the damage I've done,
A chasm of distance, two hearts undone.
I vow to change, to be a better man,
To cherish and support, hand in hand.

I'll be the rock, the shelter you seek,
A haven of love, in which we'll speak.
No longer will I ignore your pain,

Together, we'll heal, through sunshine and rain.
I'll learn to listen, to truly hear,
The depths of your joys, the weight of your tears.
Your voice, your words, they'll shape my soul,
Each syllable, a bridge to make us whole.

For love demands our growth, our self-reflection,
To mend what's broken, with true affection.
And so I promise, my dearest, to realign,
My heart and actions, with love's design.

But know, dear one, change is not overnight,
It's a journey we'll embark on, side by side.
I'll stumble and fall, but I'll rise anew,
For my love for you is steadfast and true.

I offer my hand, with love unfeigned,
To walk this path, our hearts regained.
Together, we'll mend the broken past,
And build a love that forever will last.

So, forgive me, love, this heartfelt plea,
For the pain I caused, I deeply decree.
I'm changing, growing, becoming better,
To be the man you've always sought to treasure.

With open arms and an open heart,
I'll mend the wounds, rebuild what's apart.
Let us embrace, with hope rekindled,
My love for you, forever unbridled.

This apology, my dear, binds us anew,
With gratitude for the patience, you've imbued.
May our love, like phoenix, rise from the ash,
Built on trust, in each other, abiding and steadfast.

Lose It All

It's hard to find my purpose
Tired of trying to prove I'm worth it
Time is slipping and it's urgent
I don't want to lose it all

Why Can't We?

Why can't we go out, like we used to?
Dance our heart out, like we used to?
Come home late, like we used to?
Why can't we be young, like we used to?

Why don't we look, like we used to?
Feel as confident, like we used to?
Dress in our Sundays best, like we used to?
Why don't we give it all, like we used to?

Why can't we communicate, like we used to?
Lift each other up, like we used to?
Give each other trust, like we used to?
Why can't we LOVE, like we used to?

Ministry of Presence

2 7 years young, but learned a lifetime of lessons
On the edge of life and death, I hear the chorus from the Heavens
Loved ones try to offer advice, but I need a hand from the reverend
Future up for grabs but I only want what is destined

Ain't no loss like when you lose your best friend
Haven't left my bed for 2 weeks, feeling like a dead man
Giving it all I got, I'm tired of feeling like I'm less than
Screaming at God, asking what's next then

Don't want to come off to forward, just trying to see the projections

Half a Man

When I look at you, I see light
There's a special sparkle in them brown eyes
I see your soul glistening in the sunshine
I don't know how I made you mine

I hear passion in your words
I sense patience on your mind
I feel warmth in your heart
I smell love lingering in the sky

But how can I love you, if I'm a broken man?
I have bruises, scraps, and cuts
Because I ran with my heart in my hands

Spent endless nights crying
Because I hate who I am
Not worthy of love you see
I'm a lonely wondering man

My Promise

In the depths of my soul, I find disgust,
For how I've used others, in selfish lust.
To fill the void within, I sought their love,
But caused them pain, with no thought thereof.

I see now the damage that I've done,
Using girls to fill a void, that I shunned.
I carry the weight of my selfish ways,
And vow to mend the hurt, from those past days.

I'll uncover the broken pieces within,
So that I can love with a heart that's whole and keen.
I seek redemption, to make amends,
And learn to love, without causing pain again.

Section 6
Life's Bittersweet Tapestry

Time Alone

Spent some time alone
Noticed that's where doubt, regret, and anxiety calls home
Ultimately afraid of our thoughts, even though we brag about, "how much we've grown."

Spent some time alone
Stepped into my comfortability, had to get into another zone
Reversed the wheel, rewrote the script, that our ancestors told

Spent some time alone
Developed healthy habits, new coping mechanisms, foreign traditions that I now call my own.

We have to be comfortable with being uncomfortable, because that's the only way we'll grow. We are too grown to be stuck in our way, standing in our path, and pushing back our goals.

Build It Up/Break It Down

Build for a bit, then tear that shit apart
Told you not to fall in love with me
If I can't give you all the attention you need
My toxic trait is, I've had a lot of girls fall to their knees
And I can only give you what you want, if you beg me please

Warned you so many times, about me
Now you all surprised, cause I'm changing everything
Can't ride with you, if we are on different teams
Don't misconstrued my words, trying to find the positives in
what I mean

Can't Be Trusted

You know I can't be trusted, but you just had to rush it.
Put the love up in the bag, yeah just like we rehearsed.
Thought, "this one's going to last!" I guess I kind of
cursed it.

I wrote your name across the sky, in cursive.
But we didn't see eye to eye, or vice versa.
Felt like everything we been through, was for a bigger
purpose.

You know I can't be trusted.

Youth

She said that it's fun
But we are so young
We can't get too serious
We've only just begun

Eternity

I catch myself saying I miss you, under my breathe
Been through too much it's hard to process
Stomach full of all the regrets
Feel like I haven't said everything that needed to be said
There's still a lot on my chest

There's a certain pain when I hear your name
Since you left, I haven't slept the same
Every time I close my eyes, I see your face
No longer want to play this silly game

Don't want to waist my time, I'd rather fall in love
I'm going to need you to take the lead, because I don't want
to do too much
Ready to dive right back in, but I don't want you to feel
rushed
Only been a few weeks, but it feels like several months

Last time I felt like this, I fucked it all up
Eternity will never be enough
I need an endless type of love
Is that too much?

How Do You Lie

Tell me, how do you lie?
The world full of truths, but you put on a disguise
The earth starts to crack, so you have to choose a side
Tough girl but the tears are coming, and we both know you're
about to cry

Tell me, how do you lie?
Soft girl era, but you can't seem to put your pride to the side
Screaming you don't need a man, but we both know that's a lie
Cause we both know when we fucking, is the only time you feel
alive

Tell me, how do you lie?
The boat starts sinking, so we running out of time
You on the board, I'm in the water cause I'm trying to save your
life
It's a do or die when it's you and I

So tell me, why do you lie?

All Love But No Peace

Mixed with distance and desire
Faithful but always guarded
A treasure concealed with many obstacles
Countless journeys all the same

Successful with attachment issues
Visionary yet the vision is distorted
Hard shell but creamy treat inside
All in one, or one and all the same

Sex, lust, desire
Sex, communication, trust
Sex, laughs, cuddles
Sex, sex, sex

All love but no peace

This Szn

Toxic treatment, is all we receiving
Seems like we stuck in that season
Some of us can't stop dreaming
Thoughts of our past, is the goals we're achieving

Most of us want to stop breathing
Caught in a void where we be sleeping
Stuck in this cage of life, there's no releasing
Oh, how I love this season

A Place Only We Go

Where the mist sits on the edge of sunlight.
Where the crawdads sing a song we haven't learned yet.
Where our touch calls for hyper-vigilance.

When light kisses the dark.
When life brings hope to a barren field.
When one paints the beginning of a certain ending.

Who lies in the void, but dreams of hope.
Who bellows on the mountain of desire.
Who loves but loses, and still loves the same.

A place we've been, a place only we go.

U & I

I don't believe life ends, because when I dream I fly
Been down so long, but tonight I feel alive
Life was moving so fast, you caught me by surprise
Didn't know what I envisioned before, but now it's just you and
I.

Held this pain, since that man blacked my momma's eye
No time to reflect, she said that's just a part of life
Tears only fall when I close my eyes

It's all different now, because I just created a new life
Counting down the days, I can't wait to have you in my sight
If something happens to me, just remember it's forever you and
I.

You

In every moment that has passed
In every moment that is present
In every moment that is to come
It's you

Memory Foam

When I'm falling, is the only time I feel alive
Thought we were climbing but now I'm tumbling, and I don't see you by my side
Because there's a difference between when you calling me fine, now you drawing line
The memory didn't form I guess

I feel so empty in this life, you were the only thing that gave me more
Thinking of those nights, watching the ocean crash the shore
So much done change, got you so unsure
Had you stuck when I asked, "do you love me anymore?"

The clock has struck, ain't much we can change anymore
Had me on my knees, begging baby please, shit hit me to my core
Rip my heart out, make it messy, cause I know you like the gore
The memories done stuck, the foam has set, the love is no more

Chasing

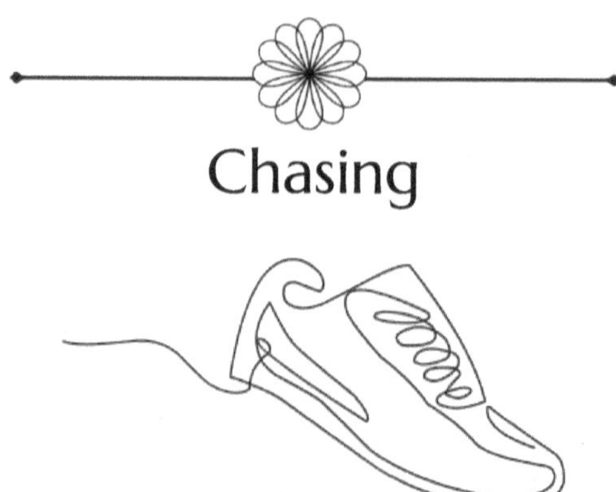

You have it once, and you never stop chasing it
Squeeze too hard, then you end up breaking it
The sad truth is there's no use in saving it

We lost it, now we waste time recreating it
It looks similar but the color quickly fades in it
The storm so prominent, it washes away any trace of it

Was it real or was my head just making it?
Are these real tears or am I just faking it?
I guess it's my fault, should have never tasted it

Time

Time disappears on you. A moment is created, and then it's gone. You never have that moment back, only the memory. You replay it over and over again, wishing you could feel that moment again. To breathe that air again, be in that space again, existing then once more.

Somewhere Else

Only see them visions late at night
Something enchanting between those thighs
On the battlefield with love
And my heart is on the line

You might be angelic
But I could never make you mine
All you had to do was open your eyes
It was written in the signs

No, no don't you cry
I promise I never lied
You were always so damn shy
Did you ever stop and wonder why?

I know I'm stuck in my pride
Deserving love, but watch it walk by
I may be here tonight
But my heart is stuck in another life

Section 7
Souls Intertwined

Eternal Love

My love feels like a warm bubble bath
Taste like chocolate kisses
Sounds like Boys To Men
Looks like forever with you

On the bad days...

It feels like long hot showers
Taste like dark chocolate
Sounds like crickets in the bedroom
Looks like a complicated math equation

My love comes with both, highs and lows
Comes with learning curves
Laughs that take the air out of your lungs
Walls that we'll have to get around
Memories that stick to your heart like glue

My love is complicated, liberating, challenging, eternal. Love
so strong, that it makes the hair on your soul stand up.

My love is whole, my love is me

Jump into My Arms

Fuck what it was, this what it is right now
Don't want no one else next to me
I feel my skin rise when you caressing me
Only you bring out the best in me

Fuck what it is, where we going
Jumped on board, now we steady flowing
Spending hours laughing, we on the same motion
Late nights spent diving in your ocean

Fuck where it's going, this shit is continuous
storm through any weather
Name tatted on my neck, because I apply the pressure
No matter what it was, is or going because this love last
forever

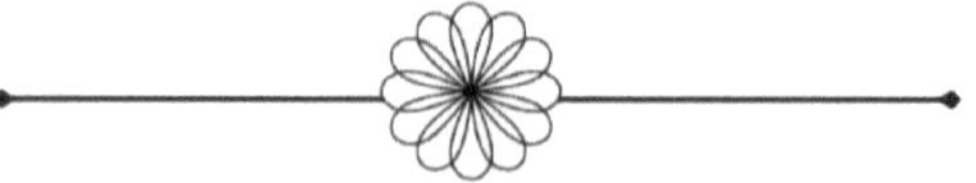

Gets Me Like You Do

Who else will introduce themselves as my blessing?
Get fired up watching Hallmark movies like you
Need my reassurance 100x a day and 200x a night
Who else gets me like you do?

Who else knows when to force me to eat before the day ends?
Give me space when I'm in my head
Tell me I'm being stupid when I want to give up
Who else gets me like you do?

Who else could make me smile from ear to ear?
Perform concerts on FaceTime in my Pjs
Have me gossiping to my momma, about how blessed I am
Who else could make me love, like you do?

For the Rest of Our Lives

Can we decorate our home, for every season?
Can we take cute holiday photos with our pets?
Can we make scrapbooks of our favorite moments?

For the rest of our lives.

Can we have dance parties in our living room?
Can we drink wine on Wednesdays and watch Vampire Diaries?
Can we make dinner together, even though I'm a terrible cook?

For the rest of our lives.

Can we be vulnerable with each other, no matter how bad it is?
Can we be patient with each others growth?
Can we build this life together, from the ground up?

For the rest of our lives, please?

Love Like My Own

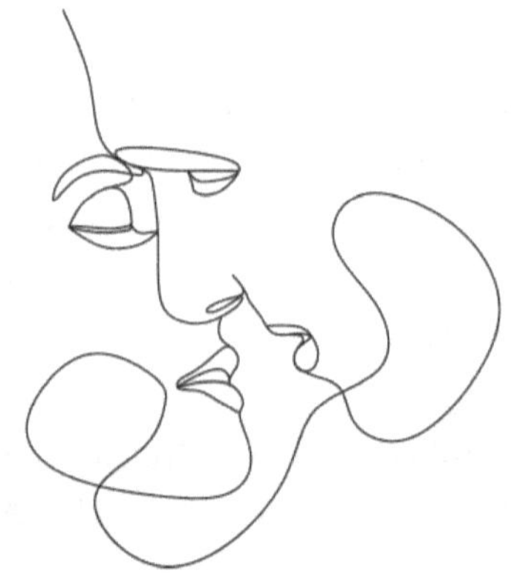

I love her like my own
I storm the castle
She takes the throne

I love her like my own
I have her heart
She is my home

I love her like my own
Wherever she goes
That's where I go

I love her like my own
That's why it feels so cold, now that I'm alone
Can't plant yourself in dry soil, and still expect to grow
Who's supposed to take care of the garden, when nobody's home?
Time shows you the weight of someone, when their finally gone

At Least We Tried

When you left me with so many questions, how was I suppose to try.
The story already told, you can see it written in the sky.
I get all my answers, when I get between those thighs.

I knew this love was real, when I had to watch you cry.
Why is it the truth only comes out, when we're on opposite sides?
How can there be a winner, when we both know we lied?

Started out with peace, all we caught was the vibe.
The journey is only beginning, so I guess we have to say our goodbyes.
It's like Givēon said, "At least we tried."

What Would You Do

What would you do for love?
Would you share your fries, even though they said
they weren't hungry?
Would you stay up all night talking on the phone, even
though you both work in the morning?

What would you do for love?
Would you share the deepest parts of you,
even if you don't know how they will react?
Would you be receptive of the deepest parts of them, no
matter what is shown?

What would you do for love?
Would you work on facing the demons,
you locked in a closet never to be opened?
Would you take a chance at forever,
even though forever isn't promised?

What would you do for love?

I Wanna Love

I wanna love, that makes me act up.
I'm talking, doing a thousand splits in the club.
Hand stands to the sunset, and nightly shoulder rubs.
I wanna love.

I wanna love, where scars get worshipped.
I'll be quiet while I listen to all things that hurt you.
Grab my hands, look into my eyes, and know I'll always be there to support you.
I wanna love.

I wanna love, that shakes my unconsciousness and tells it to wake up.
Patching our own pieces, smiling at each other. Thinking about where we are, compared to where we came from.
I wanna love.

Needed Me

She said I'm savory not sweet
Prefers dirty martinis not neat
Loves morning sex with no sheets

I don't drink liquor I smoke weed
Stuck in deep thoughts of poetry
She is my favorite thing to eat

I pull and she squeeze
She bites and I bleed
I needed her more than she needed me

Left On Read

I told her that she do too much, and she said I don't do enough. Guess it's just all in my head.
We fighting, she's biting, it all leads to the bed.
Baby can we slow it up? We don't need to rush, it's all apart of the plan.

I start to stay out late, now she hates all my friends.
We can tear those walls down, because I know we're both tired of playing defense.
We don't have to fight, I just want to do you right. Can we just play pretend?

No bickering, no fussing, no fighting.
Just you as my woman and me as your man?
...And she left me on, "read."

I Don't Want To

I don't want to love anymore
Feels like my heart is no longer pure
Spent too many nights crying on the floor
Just for us to create distance, tell me what was it for?

I don't want to love anymore
It's not that I can't, it's just not worth fighting for
Giving someone else the key, to touch my core
Now I'm getting defensive, because she found out where the trauma is stored

I don't want to love anymore
Had to double back, but now I'm finally sure
I can't stand the lying anymore
The senseless fighting anymore
I ain't hiding anymore
No sense of denying anymore

I don't want to love anymore

Magnificent

Dear lord, this life has been magnificent
Bright lights and deep pain, carry the same lessons
Powering through uncertainty, seems to be the only time we feel our blessings

Small boy with big dreams, lived a life that was hectic
Went from climbing tall trees, to climbing mountains and conquering seas
That boy was so reckless

Yearned for danger, but loved pretty things and wild dreams, and everything in between
Watched his mom work her ass off, so he told himself, "One day he'll give her everything."
Nice car, and big house that looks ever so enchanting

Well that boy turned into a man, and accomplished all his dreams
Fought demons, gains scars, and took on anything
Now he reflects, trying to understand what it's supposed to mean
All he knows, is GET IT BY ANY MEANS

Dear lord, this life has been magnificent

I Miss Me Too

I Understand Now

Before, I couldn't figure it out
Every decision plagued with doubt
Emotions pressing against my vocal cords, I wanted to shout

I should have calmed down before I let them words out my mouth
I guess that was my way of acting out
You looked so confused, trying to figure out what it was all about

I guess your love for me caught a draught
Running around my garden, looking for the spout
My heart was so back and forth, throughout

I understand now

MAN

Greatest strength, yet quickest temper
Where higher beings, fall to lesser men
Simple strokes of paint, create finer detail
Will his cells split like a seam, under the microscope?

Brothers in Christ, but enemies at war
Where blades collide, yet the heart is the affected
Betrayal not from thy enemy, but from where he sleeps
Will the demons swallow him, if he does not move?

Warrior when the sun rises, but lover nonetheless
Where victory meet's defeat, from a woman's lips
Tender in nature, yet cold where their pulse beats
Will he fall victim to his insecurities, and lose love?

Dear April

You're my favorite season
Your winds bring back the meaning
Standing alone but love is what I'm feeling

Dear April
Let's see how far it'll take you
Thought I held you soft, didn't mean to break you
Took much more than I had to save you

As fast as the wind blows, she'll grace you
Running out of breath trying to pace you
Guess I was moving too fast, didn't mean to race you

Dear April
No matter where life takes you
I hope love always embrace you

Prayers

I can't love myself so I hope the lord loves me

About the Author

Dellavonte Hune, born and raised in Madison, WI, found solace in writing amidst a tumultuous childhood that shaped his passion for storytelling. His journey from foster care to the Marine Corps, where he served for 4 years and traveled extensively, inspired his literary exploration of personal experiences. After his honorable discharge in 2021, Dellavonte penned his debut book "The After" in 2022, a poignant reflection on healing past traumas that resonated with readers worldwide. As an Amazon best-selling author, he used his platform to speak at schools and inspire others with his story. Alongside his literary pursuits, Dellavonte is dedicated to education, pursuing multiple degrees while balancing fatherhood to his newborn son, Ezekiel Hune-Moss. A committed community leader, he chairs the Personal & Professional Development Committee at the Urban League of Greater Madison Young Professionals, embodying resilience, creativity, and a spirit of service in all facets of his life.